"Hilda has a profound understanding of a great many spiritual traditions, especially Judaism and yoga."

— *Jewish Post and News*

"In a global reality where so many are feeling anxious, isolated, and overwhelmed, stopping to reflect on one of Smith's guided meditations could be just the thing for settling frayed nerves." — *Alberta Jewish News*

"Hilda Chasia Smith exemplifies all the spiritual qualities of a limitless soul — great intelligence, love, and compassion in all of her words and actions. The atmosphere Hilda generates is like heaven on Earth, as if a goddess from Above chose to walk and teach among us. One would do very well to learn meditation and spirituality from Hilda Chasia Smith."

— Rabbi Alan Green

"The kindness and frequency of Chasia's voice is a point of focus for healing energy and wisdom. She brings a sum total of pleasure and draws you into your future with her presence. These poems and meditations from a daughter of Holocaust survivors bring story, understanding, struggle, and a subsequent love of life."

— Julian Hobson, Hypnotherapist

"Hilda Chasia's artistic talent and her knowledge both of Judaism and other ancient paths of spirituality and faith make her a powerful resource in matters of the soul. I am so glad she is sharing a portion of that talent and insight with us through this work."

"Beautiful meditations and I especially love the Jewish meditations. Excellent production and sound quality on the audiobook version."

— Val Campbell, Theatre Artist

"Jewish sources teach of the simultaneous importance of knowledge, understanding, and wisdom, and Hilda Chasia Smith is the living embodiment of all three. Thoroughly rooted in Jewish texts and culture, she is one of our community's most deeply educated Jews. As a teacher, mystic, and poet, she exhibits in word and deed a true grasp of the values of our people. And, most important, her kindness, love, and passion convey a wisdom that is a priceless treasure for all who meet her. Her song sings to our hearts, and she is truly a blessing."

— Rabbi Mark Glickman

"Being a professional artist (painter), the natural rhythm of my life is to constantly pursue creativity through my work and especially friendships. Hilda Chasia is a true "original" in terms of her enormous artistic talent in many disciplines. Her passion, insight and intelligence is a unique and special gift."

— Paul Van Ginkel, Artist

"For those of us who are interested in a heartfelt journey and experiencing expanded consciousness Hilda Chasia Smith has artistically created a vehicle that is a must ride."

— Dr. Dennis Lamothe, Psychologist

CHASIA'S ENCHANTMENT

Meditations • Poems • Inspirations

CHASIA'S ENCHANTMENT

Meditations • Poems • Inspirations

HILDA CHASIA SMITH

UpRoute
Books & Media

An Imprint of
Durvile Publications

Calgary, Canada

UpRoute Books

UPROUTE IMPRINT OF DURVILE PUBLICATIONS LTD.

Calgary, Alberta, Canada
durvile.com

LIBRARY AND ARCHIVES CATALOGUING IN PUBLICATIONS DATA

Chasia's Enchantment: Meditations, Poems and Inspirations
Smith, Hilda Chasia, author
Shyba, Lorene, editor

1. Mindfulness & Meditation
2. Canadian Poetry | 3. Canadian Art

Every River Literary Series

ISBN: 978-1-988824-53-6 (print pbk)
ISBN: 978-1-988824-54-3 (e-book)
ISBN: 978-1-988824-55-0 (audiobook)

Cover painting and paintings throughout the book: Hilda Chasia Smith
Cover and book design: Lorene Shyba

Durvile Publications would like to acknowledge the financial support of
the Government of Canada through Canadian Heritage Canada Book Fund
and the Government of Alberta, Alberta Media Fund.

Canada   Alberta
                  Government

Printed in Canada. First edition, second printing. 2021.

Chasia's Enchantment is dedicated to
my beloved husband Lenny,
our precious daughters
Penny Michelle and Mandy Brooke, and to our
grandsons whom we love and adore,
Caleb Paige and Zane Rowan.

CONTENTS

PREFACE

T͟HIS BOOK, *Chasia's Enchantment* evolved when my publisher friend Lorene Shyba said, "Hilda Chasia, it's time we did a book." We worked together to develop this book of poetry and meditations that integrates my knowledge and experience on the subjects of Judaism, Kabbalah, yoga, and meditation. These have been a major part of my life as a universal soul; as a multidisciplinary teacher, an artist, and musician.

The meditations in Part I of the book are meant to be listened to for full appreciation. You will see a QR code and web address at the top of many of the pages that link to audio/video presentations of the meditations. (As an alternative, you could always get someone to read the meditations out loud to you.) The poetry, along with the meditations, are also available as an audiobook, and my paintings can be seen in colour on the website at durvile.com. We have brought together a full multimedia experience.

Judaism in this Lifetime

Judaism was what I was born into in this lifetime, coming from a modern-observant home in Winnipeg and raised by survivors of the Holocaust — my birth parents, my grandmother, uncles and aunt. I was flooded with love and affection, but also with rules and expectations to be a good student, a caring, loving young woman, and an educated person. Torah, at the heart of all Judaic practice, taught me to share the joy and reverence of a divinely inspired life. Knowing how much suffering people go through to live a good life in spite of tragedy, setbacks, and bumps in the road, along with the messages I received pragmatically and mystically interwove into the person that I have become. You see, we all come into this world unconditionally, yet circumstances, placement, and timing play a large role in what we perceive and become habituated to.

My birth was two months early, and one that could have cost my mother's life, or mine. Thankfully we both made it, and three-and-a-half years later, my beautiful sister Debbie Ellen (Elka Dvorah) was born and became my forever playmate, confidant, and friend. My grandmother, who was a midwife, a mystic, a learned and observant Jewish woman was also a major centre of my life.

Alongside my spiritual nature, I was always taught the pragmatics of life through shared responsibility and duties. Culturally and traditionally, my family celebrated all the Jewish holidays and did their best to live by the Ten Commandments of Torah. Kabbalah teachings were imbued by action of caring for others, in the family, in community and beyond.

These lessons, together with the observation and experience of people from many other cultural and ethnic backgrounds, including Indigenous Peoples, ignited the spark of divinity even further within my soul. Actually when grandmother, Bubba as I called her, had me in a stroller at about two years old, I remember being in a park, looking up at the sky and feeling a connectedness to nature and myself and to my grandmother, to everything and everyone. I did not have the words to express this heavenly/earthly enchantment then, but as life unfolded, experiences, education, travel, marriage and family expanded my use of words to express and explain soul work.

Sharing My Life's Work
The meditations and poems in this book have been chosen from a vast number of poems and aphorisms that I have been creating for decades. Through this labour of love, *Chasia's Enchantment* book and audio-book, I strive to convey feelings and inspirations to uplift your soul, and in doing so, I uplift my own. In continuing to remember the love, the Godliness, the divinity and humanity of this world, I offer you a gateway into your own peacefulness, serenity, healing, joy, and personhood.

May the poetry, the meditations, the art and music allow you to relax a little more into yourself (repeat as necessary). Within this work are Torah teachings, Vedic teachings, Kabbalah insights, meditation splendour and guidance—whatever it takes to spread and shine your own light. We never know where life will take us. Our joy of expressing, observing, learning and creating, in our love of family, and exploring the world opens us to loving opportunities.

The child in me sees the child in you. The adolescent in me sees the adolescent in you. The ever-becoming adult in me sees the adult in you. It is through my experiences that these poems and meditations have emerged. In my workshops and private sessions with people, I have found joy in seeing people relax and learn certain skills for their awakened wellbeing, and it is my hope that the words in this book will serve the same purpose.

When I give workshops or talks, I am often asked if I have books or recordings and I am delighted that the universe brought me to this moment of being able to offer this published work.

Chasia's Enchantment is an invitation for you to become more of who you are, through the breath of Torah, Kabbalah, yoga, meditation and other world teachings. Dip authentically into that awareness each time you find a poem that speaks to you. May you keep cultivating your own enchantment in love, and with blessing.

— *Shalom and Namaste,*
Hilda Chasia Szternfeld Smith (2020)

Durvile.com/Meditations.html

For guided meditations,
scan with QR app.

youtu.be/zwkaXjjghzk

For artwork in colour,
scan with QR app.

PART I
MEDITATIONS

Let us all be awakened to our
maximum potential of each moment,
leading with our spirit and inviting intuition,
along with gathered information,
so that we may respond
with a deeper presence to each moment.

Namaste. Shalom.

THE DOLPHIN

Let's go on a little journey, a guided mediation to relax and refresh you, in every cell. Let's go for a walk by the ocean. It's a beautiful day—warm, the sand is warm. The waves are dancing, and you've come to this ocean. Sit down and relax. Take a nice slow breath in, and a slow breathe out, as you relax your shoulders. Sit nice and straight as you listen to the beautiful waves as they play, allow yourself to relax even more with each beautiful inhale, and exhale. Imagine, that you have turned into a beautiful dolphin, and that you have entered this magnificent ocean filled with fish, and beautiful shells, and tiny little creatures of the ocean, dancing all around you. And you find there is a whole school of dolphins who have invited you to come and swim with them in the beauty of the deep blue ocean. And every dolphin is expressing their joy with their squeals and you are a part of it all. The sun is shining brilliantly on the ocean and the waves are dancing with you. And as you are sitting on the shore imagining that you are that beautiful dolphin playing in the water, you can feel that you *are* one... breathing the air, in and out, gently. And a smile widens on your own lips at the shore as you breathe in and you breathe out, feeling every cell in your own body, as alive and as happy, and as joyful as the imagining of you, as a dolphin. Breathe in, deeply and slowly. Breathe out, deeply and slowly. With each breath, feel the energy of the ocean, in you. For you are the ocean of your own being. Simply breathe. And when you are ready, in your incredibly relaxed state of joy and being, put your hands to your heart, bowing to the ocean within you, the ocean in the world, all the oceans, and know that we are all a part of this magnificent universe, like the dolphins in the ocean.

Namaste. Shalom.

THE WHITE FEATHER

Repeat the beauty of breathing, slowly and deeply. Can you feel the difference between the air going in, and the air coming out? You might find a difference in the temperature, and smile in gratitude to this moment. Can you imagine stepping into a beautiful forest in the summertime? The trees are in full foliage and flowers of every colour are gently blowing in the wind, colours of the rainbow and beyond, fluttering their petals as if to say, "Welcome, so glad you are here." As you step into the forest, there is a beautiful pathway in front of you, a wide pathway of soft golden earth as if to way, "Come, come deeper into the forest." As you take a step you feel that the sun rays are falling even more enchantedly onto you, shedding their magnificent light all around you, as they have right through the forest. Allow yourself to walk in grace. And as you are walking, become even more aware of your breathing. Has it deepened a little bit? Allow it to. Let your lips turn into a radiant smile and know that you are part of the magic of life, of all this radiance. And as you are walking on the path, it turns to the right and you wonder. But allow yourself in that wonder to be carried by the path to wherever it is going. And as you look at the beautiful trees and the magnificence of the blue sky, you feel a soft warm breeze at your back. Suddenly, you hear the sound of water as you walk through the spendour of the forest. Butterflies and birds are dancing and singing. You can see them in the distance. A few butterflies have circled you in the joy of knowing you are there. As the water gets a little louder, you can see a river flowing and you walk to the edge of the beautiful bank of the river. As you look down to the river, you see a large white feather that is there in front of your feet. The lightness of the feather seems to magically rise and you reach your hand out and the feather lands right in your hand. This feather is a reminder of the lightness of your own being as you listen to the water sing a soft melody, you can feel the refreshment of your own heart and soul in every cell of your body radiating with this new energy and the reminder of the lightness of your own breath and your own being, for you are that. You return, feeling totally refreshed and at ease with the lightness of being that is beyond words as you walk back through the forest. Ageless child, you are a part of this magnificent world and universe and all that you are is within and around you. Let your spirit soar and as you hear those words, you open your arms with a feather in your hand, and slowly raise them as if you are an eagle and bring them down, standing firmly on the ground, moving in silence, bringing your hands to your heart with the feather. Knowing that you are safe, that you are whole, that you are loved, that you are strong. Remember, you are the river, you are the forest, you are the sky, you are the earth, you are everything. In the forest, may you be ever green all of your days, soaring like an eagle, with your feet planted firmly on the ground. *Namaste. Shalom.*

SHALOM

This is a Jewish meditation. A meditation from the words of our Siddur that is read in the morning, in the evening, in the afternoon. This is a prayer thanking the divine and asking for peace for all Jews and all people in the world.

Oseh Shalom beemromahv
Hoo ya-aseh shalom alainu
vay uhl kol Israail v'eemru omain

May the one who brings peace to His universe
Bring peace to us and to all Israel.
And let us say, Amen.

Ya-ahseh shalom ya-ahseh shalom
shalom alainu v'kol ha-ansheem
v' eemru omain

Let there be peace. Let there be peace for all.
And let us say, Amen.

Durvile.com/Meditations.html

GUIDED STAR DREAM

Sit or lie down comfortably. Come with me on a journey through the stars on a beautiful clear night—a warm night in summer. Relax, breathe in, breathe out slowly, and with each breath, deepen your relaxation just a little more. As you float in the sky, allow yourself to be carried by the warm breeze and watch the stars twinkling as you breathe in the beautiful soft air, and know that you are radiating with those stars. As you breathe in and out, slowly deepen the stillness and the relaxation of your heart. And when you are ready, make your way back to your mat, your bed, or your chair — wherever you are. Wiggle your toes and your fingers. Become aware of exactly where your body is and breathe normally.

THE FEMININE DIVINE

Join me in a meditation of your feminine divine. Every person has a masculine divine and a feminine divine. In the ancient teachings of both Sanskit and in Judaism, Sanskrit being a holy language of the Hindu people, and Lashon Kodish a Hebrew holy language of the Jewish people, we find Shakti, the feminine divine and Shekhinah, the feminine divine. The feminine divine is universal. Let us go on a journey of embracing the feminine divine within you, and me. Sit comfortably on a chair or on a mat, whatever it is you'd like to sit on — even a comfortable big rock, with your back nice and straight, with your head resting on your beautiful shoulders. Relax your shoulders. Lift your sternum towards the sky. Simply breathe, with your mouth closed, breathe in the fresh beautiful air around you that is constantly circulating in you, and back out into the world. With each breath, allow yourself to simply relax a little more. Imagine, that there is a beautiful light, a golden light in the centre of your heart and that light is permeating through your whole body. Watch it expand through every limb, from your feet, moving right through your legs, as you breathe slowly and deeply, feel that light warming you, gently. Feel that light, like a ball of light moving into your hips and into your lower abdomen, and all of your body, moving upward into your belly, into your heart again and into every organ and every part of your body. This light is illuminating you. There is the possibility of manifestation of whatever it is you that you need for health, wellness, prosperity, joy, connection, communication, peace, love, equanimity. And this light is moving into your throat, all the way again through your face, between your eyes, all the way through the crown of your head. And as you breathe in and out, feel the blessing of your breath, a gratitude for being able to breathe and being breathed by the divine. Of all that manifests and is manifested — feel the the Shekhinah, and Shakti, the feminine divine of your own personal gender and awareness of who you are in the universality of your being. And imagine yourself now allowing a waterfall that suddenly appears in a beautiful mountain that you can imagine pouring all that beautiful energy, warmly, onto you. As you stand beneath the waterfall, whether you are dressed or whether you are in a bathing suit, or whether you have come there in your own skin, letting the water shine on you in the sunshine. Let all that needs to be washed away wash away on your body as you feel the sun. And the strength of the mountain, the presence of her healing surrounding you. The feminine divine within the mountain, within the earth, in water and within you, allowing yourself to feel refreshed and knowing that all is manifested is from the womb of life and choose that which brings you home to Mother Earth, that brings you to the Shakti, to the Shekhinah of who you are. See yourself coming right back to this moment on your chair or the big rock you might be sitting on, wherever you are, in the calmness of your beautiful breath, smile to your heart. Close your eyes, breathe gently for a minute or two, and open your eyes as if for the very first time. Peace, Shakti, Shekhinah.

Durvile.com/Meditations.html

SLEEP, DEREKH THE WAY

Join me in a guided meditation that may help you go to sleep more easily, more restfully. Sit down on a chair with your feet on the floor, or lie down on the ground or on your bed. Feel the earth beneath you and simply rest. Be able to breathe into your beautiful body a gift of air flowing in and flowing out, rhythmically, naturally. With your eyes closed, allow the music to bring just a little more quiet to you. With every breath to simply relax and sink more deeply into your own being. Let all the thoughts of the day float away like a cloud passing by, or a wave on the ocean that returns to the stillness of the ocean. Keep breathing slowly and deeply, allowing yourself to feel the beauty of your heartbeat. And when you are ready, let's find our way to the beauty of our hearts, you to yours, and me to mine, simply through the *derekh*, the way. Starting with your feet, allow yourself to feel, the best you can, the inside of your feet. Allow them to relax, completely. Moving to your ankles, feel the inside of your ankles relaxing, as we are all covered in this amazing encapsulating skin that supports everything inside. Feel your calves in the front of your legs relax completely. Moving to your knees, allow your knees to relax even more, doing nothing but imagining a deeper relaxation. Moving to your hips, feel them melt into the floor or the chair that you are sitting on. With each breath, allow yourself to simply be. If thoughts come to you, ideas, just let them float away for now and be with your magnificent breath. Relax your abdomen, feel yourself getting even more relaxed. Keep breathing deeply, and softly. Let your ribcage relax, in the front and in the back, knowing that every organ is relaxing and filling your body with rest, as you breathe into your body, and out. And as we make our way to our heart, feel a beautiful glowing light, expanding into every part of your body and you've made your way home to your heart, but you travel with that light now to your throat as your heart keeps expanding the light within you everywhere in the loving gracious fullness of your restfulness for that is the way of the *derekh*. And the light now fills your face and your ears and moves right to the top of your head as you melt even further into peacefulness, relaxation and the true beauty of who you are, in every breath. Take a nice deep breath and feel all of your body relaxing even deeper into the earth as you are supported above and below on the way on the *derekh* of life, always leading with your heart wrapped in the soul of life, wrapped in your own soul. *Laila Tov*. Good Night.

PART II
INSPIRATIONS

We have listened to our souls' messages.
Open the gateway to your heart sweet child.
Enter into the kingdom of all that awaits you.
Your eternal soul is calling each of you to surrender
to love in the here and now
with compassion, gratitude,
grace and abundance.

Shine your heart light as
love surrenders you to
all that is, all that was
and all that will ever be.

Chasia's Enchantment

CHASIA'S ENCHANTMENT

Caring hearts, the abstract senses
intuition's invitation to all that is.
The six-star nations.

Oh my God and Oh my soul.
Infinite and in control.
And letting go, abundance rises,
and all that is discerned with love.

Sudden fulfillment of desire.
Curiosity, feeling flame and feeling fire.
Feeling whole, and doing this
in pure enchanted, abled bliss.

The more soul connected that we are,
it's written in a wind, a star,
and so I say imagine dreams,
imagine visions, smile and play
The infinite of every day.

THE MANY MASKS

The many masks that we present
in times of love and love's descent
are mirrored in a pool of light
that serves our journey day and night.

The light of all that ever was.
The light of all that is
is never lost in time and space.
We each receive with granted grace,
the perfect light of love divine
unmasking truth moves Earth and time.

The stance is yours, the stance is mine.
The endless possibility of every opportunity
is never lost in time or space.
We each receive with granted grace
the perfect act of love divine.

The stance is yours, the stance is mine,
this wave of rhythm, movement, gesture.
Environmental roots of Master,
Mistress of this universe,
Shakti, Shekhinah
no need at all to just rehearse.
We only need to look and see, you are that, it's true,
you're you. It's true I'm me
together in this family. Diversified humanity.

We belong to earth and sky.
How we breathe is how we fly.
Fly to wellness, fly to peace, letting go of all unease.
Gratitude, appreciation, patience, practice.
You will find delicious bliss and satisfaction,
the many masks unmasked in time.
Oh the living, so divine.
Wild wonder, you amazing child of this universe.
Ever being, every beginning,
in the endlessness of being.
We all have come a long way.
Children. Our inner child. Always with us.
No matter what we have experienced,
we can gently feel it step by step
and still remain in love with authentic being.
For this is truly love.

The decorations of life have been fun
but we know that the unity that arises
to authentic love was, is,
and always will be our birthright.
Our journeys are divine inspirations.

May we continue to let go of that
which does not serve us anymore.
Embrace, embody all that does.
May it grow and grow, lovingly, intentionally.

MERCI A DIEU

Je dis, I say
Mon coeur, my heart
Mon coeur, my heart
Toujours, toujours, always, always
Merci à Dieu, je dis, thank you to God, I say
Chaque jour la même, each day the same
Les mots sont ceux-ci, the words are these.
Merci à Dieu, merci, thank you to God, thank you
Pour toi, for you, pour tous le monde, for everyone,
Pour mon coeur, for my heart
Merci à Dieu, thank you to God
Merci à Dieu, je dis, thank you to God, I say
Merci à Dieu, thank you to God.

SPRINKLE JOY

Sprinkle joy, peace increases.
Sprinkle joy everywhere and in your sleep.
We could all use joy's sweet release.
With love in every molecule
Sprinkle joy through thoughts with ease.
Surrender to joy's endless lease.
Yes, sprinkle, sprinkle, sprinkle joy.
Sprinkle joy as much as you please.
Imagine joy in fantasies and in the real
at every meal. Sprinkle joy, sprinkle joy,
may joy, like this friend, never cease.

AGNI, THE FIRE

The *agni* fire of soul ignites the flame
that controls all roles and helps us see
the *sattva* purity of you and me.
To end *samskara*, memory of habit's wheel
without reflection might conceal
the *satya* truth to help us heal.
Like you and me, my friend, this fire glows,
inspired by life's yes's and no's.
The *agni* that fuels wellness thrives.
The *agni* of too much diminishes lives.
Anger, hunger, ego's grip
in groundless action, mind and lip.
Tamed and truthful to express
life's real passion, I confess.
How *agni's* fire passions life
so filled with guidance, lose the strife.
Feel the warmth of fire's flame
no overheating for there's no gain.
Contain life's fire to stay ignited
fueled with vision, stay delighted.
Attune, discern, unite
the empire of your gentle might.
Please your body, spirit, brain
and we can live a soul-filled plane.
Digesting food and feeling well.
Lightness of being, happiness in every cell.
Agni, the digestive fire of life.

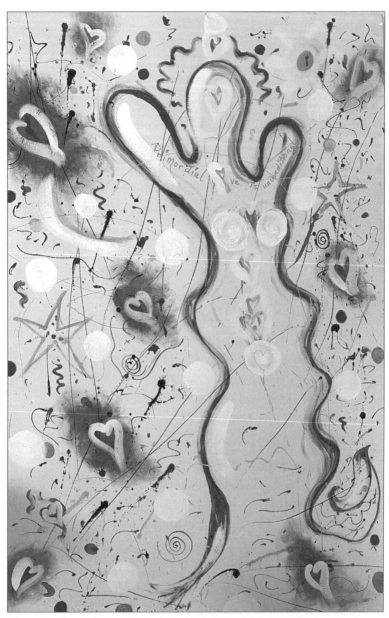

Transformations: Interiors

TRANSFORMATIONS: INTERIORS

What do you see when you look at me?
My angel wings? The dark? the light?
The bright? The dim?
What do you see when you look at me?

Butterfly rising, heart on the floor,
open and sharing, receding once more.
The depth of my being like yours
is concealed.
And all those who love us,
Help us reveal ... the God spark,
divine spark of life and of being.
Opening up to what needs to be healed
to wholeness and all that in time
is revealed.
Oh, interiors. The vastness of nature
and nature within our Godly souls and being.

Open your eyes, breathe and make space
to feel all of the presence, so blissfully freeing.
Interiors.

KABALLAH INSIGHTS

Vessels
A divine light of creation shines in everyone.
Let it shine on wisdom, experiences, in all time.
Then understanding takes its shape
when wisdom and understanding unite
creating compassion in this world.

Grace awakens with compassion.
Love and moral code, the will that teaches humanity
to not be blinded materially.
We detach, we feel no lack when grace,
compassion lived unite.
They build another gift indeed.
The mercy that we need.

Above the splendour of all consciousness
exists the point of your fine being,
knowingness in the beauty,
the true beauty of bountiful seeing.

We witness our desires, expressing feelings here.
Victory aligning them with humble grandeur
and majesty of thoughts.
God's insights into Being,
choose what serves life at best.

Resonate with life's divinity
Love fully, God's request.
The active power, God's universal frequencies,
physical, sensual, intimate, spiritual.
Pouring divine and human worlds, all soaring.
Righteous deeds fulfill this world.

Creator's presence, opportunities, leads,
life's invitation to fill our needs.
Yes, our body and our earthly senses,
Our planet, the root of the tree.
The Holy Shekhina, the presence, the lower
unites with the upper. Both count, infinitely.
Original error caused separation,
we connect, repair and reground.
Becoming aware of all we can be and
all we can share and we're found.
The Kabbalah, in all four worlds:

Archetypal—*Atzilut*
Creative—*Briah*
Formative—*Yetsirah*
Material—*Assiah*

Shalom

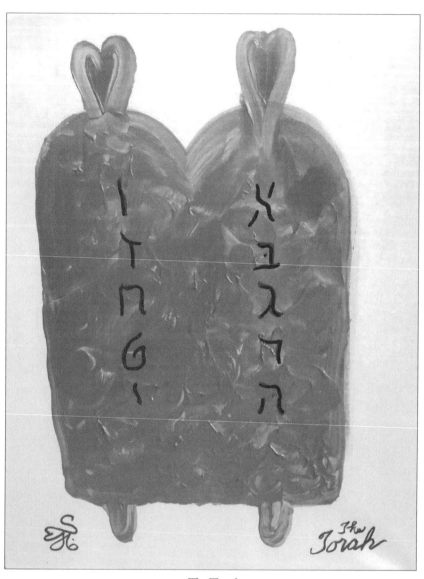

The Torah

TORAH

The golden rays on Moses' crown,
as he who holds the tablets in his arms.
The Ten Commandments containing
the six hundred thirteen mitzvot, ten ethical rules for
living and loving in holiness through life for all life.

The Jews are the Nation that were given the Torah
and the Torah brings the light of
the Torah wisdom into the world
for the world, for the love of humankind
and the awe of the divine one God
who created the world in six days
and rested on the seventh.

The golden light of divine glory, rules for living
and being through Torah, trickles down into every
human's story. Torah! Torah! Torah!

All that has been created in this universe can
be found and is still unfolding from Torah,
the teachings, almost six thousand years old.

The written law came after the oral law and the
written law has been with us for almost four thousand
years. May that which imbues every heart and soul
with glorious life keep unfolding.
And if you choose, learn a little Torah.

Torah. For one and all.

LIFE LESSON

Inwardly and outward free.
Compassion, laughter, trust emerge
in the choice of rising courage.
Mind, brain, and heart unite impart
the knowingness of answers you will find.
Torah's hidden messages trusting time
to reveal all that makes you love and heal.
Sharing timely what you feel.
Develop calmness, restful mind.

The power of our authenticity
lifts spirit, sense of being.
Remember all the storms of life subdued
simply with a shift of mood.
Vedic words *Satya*, truth; *Prema* love
blending energies above.
Kehttehr, crown,
unification's call.
Tifereht, beauty of it all,
and below to now bestow.
Malchut, foundation deep,
life's learning, oh the letting go.

Delight in all that you do know
deep inside inspires so.
Wisdom *chokhmah*, to clarify the choice
of divine love and love's voice.

Laws and attributes to heal.
Hear the call to rise and be.
Hear this call, calm naturally.
Inwardly and outward free.

TU BISHVAT
the Fifteenth of SHVAT

Happy Birthday trees,
Oh Happy New Year trees.
The rain of life has mostly ceased.
The trees begin a brand new lease
of growing buds into soft leaves and
fruits of nature, as breezes tease
and bounty meets our hearts with joy.
The trees' New Year on Tu Bishvat
Renews the hope of all we've got
to so inspire our desire, universally
to grow and stretch and truly be
as supple as a growing tree.

In Israel and in the world
to share the buds of love most fruitfully
take care of trees,
take care of all, in nature and in life.

With gratitude to God divine,
Creator's world, we share the work
and harvest the whole plentitude
of every bowl of food.
In time, in blessing.
Food for body, mind and spirit.
Raise your voice, good day, let's hear it.
Tu Bishvat's a happy time
with thankfulness to the divine.

YOGA

Yesterday today and tomorrow
is open to embrace. Gurus, sages all agree
the value of yoga philosophy.
Stretch mind and body greatly
with postures right for you.

Meditate to elevate your internal grounding
and de-stress with ease
in the practice of yoga every day, if you please.
As we work with our bodies, our minds grow in flow.
We may learn to listen more wisely
to the yes and no of our habits
and our rituals that bring much more
joy, peace and balance to our lives each day.
Our hearts rise in union in a well lived way.
Ancient wisdom brings gentle teachings
for the world to embrace.

Yoga lessons for the present,
karmic teaching in play.
Each yoga pose has a message
for your life and soul be open mainly
for the inspiration of your truth as it unfolds.
Yoga lessons work so well for the aging and the youth
the sacred, the divine, the bliss of human being
in the natural that resonates in breath
and breath's own time!

Namaste, an ancient way to healthy stay.

I BREATHE IN

I breathe. I breathe in love and life and yes, I let go of what does not serve serenity. I trust, I love, I am wholeness. Forevermore. I breathe in love and I breathe out whatever does not serve peace. I breathe in stillness, and I breathe out chaos. I breathe in opening, and I breathe out constriction. I breathe in possibility, I breathe out resistance. I breathe in joy, I breathe out lack of joy. I breathe in strength, I breathe out fear. I breathe in healing, I breathe out hurt. I breathe in Torah, I breathe out worry. I breathe in Kabbalah, I breathe out ignorance. I breathe in yoga, I breathe out senselessness. I breathe in sutras, I breathe out confusion. I breathe in Upanishads, I breathe in understanding, I breathe in the bodhi tree, I breathe out selfishness. I breathe in all teachings of all the ways of life that support life. I breathe out falsehoods. I breathe in love, I breathe out love. I breathe in support, communication, I breathe out love, creativity and forgiveness. I breathe in prosperity. I trust, I love, I am wholeness, just like you, forevermore.

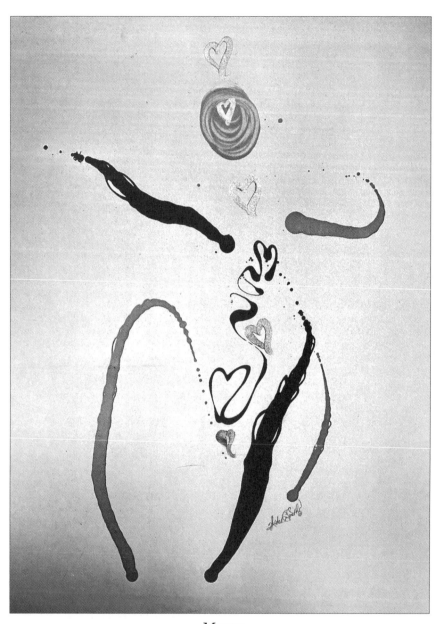

Mantra

MANTRA

Mantra.
Vehicle of the mind.
Spaciousness.
Heart's desire.
Illuminated white sun.
Oh, the planets and the surrender
to all that makes life
a meditation.

The sweet sounds manifested
from the unmanifested.
Primordial sounds.
Sounds of nature
And your own
heart beating
mantra.

SOUL TO SELF

Do not be afraid to keep stepping into the truth
of all you are. Remember to refine
your spirit, mind, and body's gifts.
Grounded in your presence.

Receive and share your individual treasures.
Your happiness, your laughter, your insight.
Your awareness, your beauty, your intuition, your focus,
your credibility, creativity and wholeness.
Express your passion, your purpose and
connect to your connection
as you continue to unfold, exquisitely
in silence, observation, or expression in life.

Your magnificence shines through your loving,
growing self-esteem.
True confidence and the surrender to your healed
and healer's gifts within you.
You are an artist of your own life.
Voicing your truth with dignity, grace.

Wild wonder, you amazing child of this universe.
Ever being, ever beginning,
in the endlessness of being.
We all have come a long way.
Children. Our inner child. Always with us.
No matter what we have experienced,
we can gently feel it step by step
and still remain in love with authentic being.
For this is truly love.

The decorations of life have been fun
but we know that the unity that arises in
our authentic love was, is,
and always will be our birthright.
Our journeys are divine inspirations.

May we continue to let go of that
which does not serve us anymore.
And embrace, embody all that does.
May it grow and grow, lovingly, intentionally.

POWER OF HOPE

Remember, the power of hope is real.
Childhood innocence that
ignites ego-less states,
removes judgment and criticism.

Lighthearted, carefree.
Play a little each day.
Accept people in the best light.
We all have our burdens.

We all are looking for solutions at times.
Sit, relax, refrain from criticizing
yourself or anybody else.
Notice, observe, let go.
People will notice you are more welcoming,
for lightheartedness is the heart of freshness.
And then hope is ready to be renewed.
We are potential, pure potential, not of what is
but all that might be.

Our potential for limitless awareness
overcomes all limitations.
Remember the power of hope is real.

RIVER OF LIFE

Forever the river of life just flows.
It turns a bend and goes and goes.
The surface changes with the mood,
calm or raging filled with food,
the oxygen of life in flow.
The river bed, unknown and known.
The rocks and shorelines, mud and sand.
The rain and sleet, the snowy land.

The stars shine down, moon's face and sun.
The river flows and says,

"Just come to fill your lungs
with nature's bliss."

And there you stand and here it is,

"Be playful, clear each day."

Anchored Play

ANCHORED PLAY

Anchored, I can play and never drift away.
But let my soul rise and let it flow,
into the stream of life's own show.
For in the play of life I see
the very real of fantasy
brought down to Earth, the vision seen
and practical made of the dream.

Focus, intention, attention, and will.
And destiny reveals itself,
Oh, the joy of anchored play.
For life says, "Play with surprise and purpose!
Come my way."

And in discernment, I can find
the affluence and openness that
guides my being and my mind.
The knowingness,
the flow of all eternal holiness,
anchored.
Once again life says,
"Come let's play."

UNIFIED SPIRITUALITY AND TRUTH

Study some Jewish Torah, Kabbalah deep codes.
Yogic and Vedic wisdom to awaken union.
Union of transits, true transits to life.
African healers and First Nation connections
are beings of light.
The Tao and Confucius are Asian and Eastern.
All of this is learning and sharing.

The Inca, the Celtic, the Toltec, the North.
The wise ones of all lives, truth knowers, deep truth.
Together we join sharing planet and space.
To repair and heal this world with
love and with grace.

All sacred teachings —
The Christians, the Muslims, the Jews
over four billion Abrahamic people
all of the others, we all need some healing.
The great and the small, sharing lifeline and all
the world according to the Torah is one narrow bridge
may we all hold hands spiritually in love
sharing this earth.

Shalom. Om. Namaste.

MINDFULNESS

Our heart eyes feel and see and we respond.
The eyes on our face just might deceive us
but not our heart eyes.

Our heart is the gateway to our spirit.
It is our soul that our heart
opens up the door to.
Our heart and our heart's eyes are
the gateway to our soul
that frees our spirit
into right action, always.

The purity that is our whole
welcomes us just as we are,
complete in the frequency and resonance
of *Chesed*, loving kindness to our true self,
children of God, in the mystery of life.

Let us surrender blissfully to this mindful practice
with attention to every moment
with our heart eyes' intention
helping to will our destiny.

THE HONEY SWEET TORAH

Honey sweet is the enjoyment,
the learning that Torah teaching brings
to every child, to every soul.
God gave the Jews the responsibility and joy to learn,
to teach to share the Torah teachings with all from
generation to generation.

Torah knowledge, faith in action, that's the call.
Mitzvot good deeds, commandments,
life's ups and downs, and turn arounds
happen on this plane.
Torah teaching help to keep
the world in love, and sane.
Tempered feelings, wisdom shows, how respect
just grows and grows.

The word is power when explained.
Anger, hurt, can all be tamed.
Righteous actions can be named.
We're only human, stop all blame.
Turn to wisdom teachings flame.
Flame of honest feelings touched.
Dare to question, welcome much.

Kabbalah is within this learning.
Books and books of understanding.
Rabbis spending lifetimes to bring clarity
to you and me through the teachings of Torah
and Kabbalah in practical spirituality lived.

Guided lessons teach us how
to stand in spirit tall.
Love for God and love for elevating life
from the mundane into the sacred.
Love for humanity, ethics and taking care of the
natural world that God created.
Using intelligence and heart
for the good of humankind
with exploration and
loving awareness revealed in its lessons.

Fingerpainting

FINGER PAINTING

God's hand and heart in everything.
The rain and sun that surely bring
the ether and the flow of water.
The elements within our flesh.
God's hand and heart in everything.

The waves of ocean, clouds and space.
The worlds within each human's face.
The abstract of each form's own grace.

The flow of life, the storm
The light.
Connection.

The pure heart and the eyes that see
the flow of loving ecstasy
The unformed and the formed, united.

Finger painting, heart to heart,
God's hand and heart in everything.

THIS MUCH WE KNOW

This much we know, that no matter how much
we know there is more to know, to understand,
to transcend to move to perfect peace.
Within ourselves, within our wondrous worlds of
blessings, healings and wholeness.

This much we know, that with every day and every night
a new beginning comes as we live here on planet Earth.

Whatever brings us just a little closer to finding answers
to our questions fills the gaps of misunderstandings into
profound honouring of each other's journey
in time, space and beyond.
This much we know, love's and life's potential
lives here in our every breath. This much we know.

WE ARE COMING TOGETHER

God alone gives me peace of mind.
Of course you are in my heart all life long.
Oh my dear God, you are in my heart.
Each breath says,
"I am here with you."
All the people I know are here with you.
God alone, God alone gives me peace of mind.
I am happy, I am filled with love from God.
This was how the world was built.
In every soul, a spark of God alone.
We are coming together from God alone.

BE KIND

Respect the omnipresent and you will acquire
an inspired passion for life.
With a foundation of openness,
one gains insight into the reasons
for the cycles of life.

From purity arises a deep desire
to protect one's body.
And from the purification of one's essence,
cheerfulness arises.
And with it, one pointed concentration,
mastery of our senses
and the capacity for sustaining
the vision of our true self.

The innocence and knowing,
the pure potential,
and the grace of embodied acceptance.
From contentment,
one gains deep supreme happiness.
Be kind to yourself,
be kind to others, body, mind and spirit.

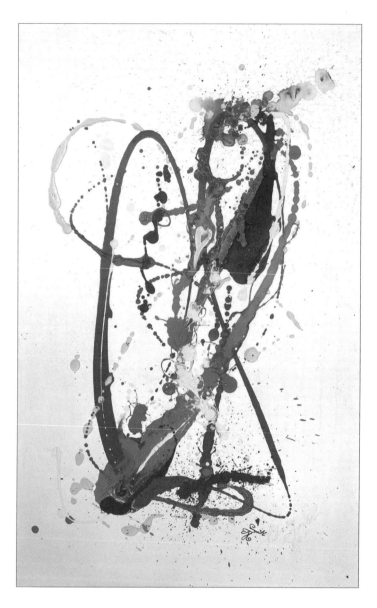

Matrix of Love

MATRIX OF LOVE

Every connection, every direction,
every selection of thought,
feeling,
emotion,
in the spaciousness
of love's coherence
guides us into the mystery,
into the magnitude
of the matrix.

Open yourself up.
Dare to be
in the matrix
of love's equanimity.

Oh, the matrix of love, of life,
of seeing, of feeling
of touching, of sensing, of being
in the matrix of love.

HOME TO YOU

In spite of any sorrow or heartache, we have held,
released, we find tomorrow a world all by itself.
Unfolding in each moment
the hope, the joy, the bliss
of everything before us
one moment at a time.

How can anybody miss the opportunities
awaiting each person on this Earth
to grow in their own story?
Each moment like a bird, a possibility unfolding.
The air upon your skin, the sunlight changing.

Every moment in the world we're in,
the beauty that's within you
could never cease to call upon the moment
that is new in every moment.

See the shawl of love and beauty
through tear-stained pillows, cries.
Wash your face, sweet darling, and empty to surprise
the incoming wisdom, the joy of who you are.
No matter what the problem
solutions are not far.
The dignity of your own heart
will bring you home to you.

LIFETALK

The lustrous beam of light I see
connects the all of you and me.
We're born into a time and place,
applaud and cheer and land and praise
the miracle of life and living,
circulating lambent giving.

Nature, God, art, science, space.
Common sense, resplendent face.
Imagination may reveal
the affluence that you conceal.

Ideas, hopes and inspiration
for the world, for every nation.
Vociferate with confidence,
uniquely you, do take a chance.

Amplify the call to love
the olive branch, the snow white dove.
Resources, we have got enough
to mine the field of heart.
That beam of light, a grand unveiling.
That's the way to start.

PRASANTA ALOKA
PEACEFUL BRILLIANCE

Prasanta aloka, peaceful brilliance.
I invite divinity, God, Creator
to flow and flood my being
With peaceful brilliance.

OM

LIVING PASSION

Cultivate joy, sharing what excites you.
Discover what ignites your passion.
Discover your true purpose.
Everyone has dharma, a special purpose in this life.
We all have unique gifts, we have unique needs.
Connecting with our dharma
allows us to express them.
What do you really, really want
and what do you really, really need?
How will you use your unique gifts and talents
to serve yourself and others?
One way to find out is to explore, try new things.
Let go of what doesn't serve you anymore.
And stay open to love, to life, to joy,
to whatever inspires you.
Living passion.

LIFE POEM

Choose to live each day midst life's
tears and woes and trials.
You will feel love's buoyancy uplifting you.
To yourself be fair and kind, and
to others you will find
that blood is flowing in your skin,
everyone is truly kin.

Bless and give by how you live.
Gentleness is strength you know.
May love guide you as you walk
endlessly in every talk
that brings through silence radiance,
the soulful whisper of this dance.
The simple things that so enhance our journey.
Oh the realms of love's own ranges.
Laugh, cry, love, and truly be.
Touch truth and then set it free.
Whatever it is, you are in the tree of life.

Exercise your loving ways.
Express your love exquisitely.
Embraceable and loveable
no matter what has happened.
Dare to dream to visualize, to sparkle
with sincerity. Step into your reality, now.
Patience, practice, real, no dress rehearsal.
Simply be. Express yourself and you will see.
In each day, most naturally.
The you you are, that shining star.

My Heart in my Hand

MY HEART IN MY HAND

My heart in my hand.
A kiss of desire.
Grounded in restful awareness.
I feel warmth of fire
igniting the *agni*, within me, this fire.

I feel my soul rising higher and higher.
Oh, infinite truth, infinite flow.
Who knows where imagination will go?
What will reveal itself in creative exposure.

In rising, fulfillment, enlightened awareness
Oh, do we dare to just be and to see
where life's road will take us?
Yes, you and me.
All of us
in this incredible dream.
My heart in my hand, enchantedly.

LOVE COMFORTS
Translation of Liebeh Traist

There comes a time
when love knows
what heart must learn.
Love comforts everyone.
Soul! Body! Mind! Spirit!
Not much needed.
Heart will hear a drop of love
just like the sun shines light,
a drop of love lights everyone,
and everywhere, for love is true.
Honey deep, magic, bliss is love's pure kiss.
Sweet and precious, love's own fire.
There comes a time when love does know
what heart must learn.
Love comforts!
Love inspires!

LIEBEH TRAIST

Ess koomt a tzeit ven leibeh vaist
vohs hartz mooz lehrnen
leibe traists alehmehn!
neshomeh! goof! mayukh! ruakh!
neesht a sukh gedarfn
hartz veht hehrn, a trop foon leibeh
poonkt vee dee zoon shynt leekht
a trop foon leibeh buhlikhts alehmehn.
oon oomehtoom, vyl leibeh eez troi
honik teef, keeshehf grestehr gleek
eez leibeh's tzeertlekh keesh
zees oon tyehr, leibeh's aign fyehr
Ess koompt a tseit ven Leibeh vaist
vohs hartz mooz lernehn
Leibeh traist! Leibeh buhgystehrt!
Leibeh traist.

The Mountain

THE MOUNTAIN

Dig deep within the mountain of your own being.
Dig deep into your own heart.
Remove anything that blocks the truth
of your own heart expanding into
the lightness of being.
Oh, the strength of mountains
in any moment can be crumbled.

But the heart of who you are
lives eternally.
For the mountain that you are
is held together by the golden light
of your soul that is embracing your heart,
and everything that is mined
is pure gold.
Pure light.

The mountain of your own heart and soul
is your glory, divinely given, and received.
Be mountain strong, and mountain life affirming.
Dig deep into your own heart.
May we all dig deep into our own hearts
and manifest great love for one another.
And the planet.

GO! GO! GO TO YOUR HEART!

Go to your heart and say,
"Ananda, Lev, teach me to love
more clearly, more deeply
by the light of all the space within me.
More space than I ever knew that I had."

Everyone has so much room
because what brought you into being
is invisible, untenable, and real.

Sound waves, atoms, molecules,
move and shape sound, touch, sight,
feelings, taste, insight, intuition,
clairvoyance, audio voyance,
extra-sensory perception.
Feelings travel in our bodies to other people.
The world herself was given to us with
signs and messages through energy fields
that we cannot see, and those we can.

Exploring the possibilities of logic,
you will find there are many things that happen
beautifully in this world that have no logic.
Love is a controlled, open freedom, happiness is an
elusive butterfly, but joy is love in action.
It is always available.

Happiness can bring joy, however, if happiness
is dependent upon anyone or anything, as most
happiness is, it is temporary.

When we feel sad or frustrated,
knowing we can feel whatever
we are truly feeling brings us joy, even in the
midst of whatever emotion is presenting itself.
There is an ecstatic stillness that is
the presence of that knowingness.
It will always bring us home.
It invites us to self-care and self-love always.
That kind of joy is a marvelous fit. Try it.
Allow your joyful memories to stay at the forefront
of your life the best you can, and the habit of
remembering them will bring you back to centre if
you get a little lost, as we all can.

Love is the answer always.
What is your question? Sit with it.
Listen to some relaxing instrumental music.
Sit with it.
Outside or inside your home,
or someplace you can mindfully see
The truth of the beauty that is you.

If that does not resonate with you,
be gentle on yourself.
Breathe, and know that life is there with you.
How do we know we are being breathed?
Who or what is breathing us?
That presence is always there.
We just forget to remember.
Go! Go! Go to your heart!

EEKH SHEEK DEER A KOOSH
I SEND YOU A KISS

Eekh sheek deer a koosh
I send you a kiss

meet leebeh oon een fryndshuhft
with love and in friendship.

doo beest azoi tyehr tsoo meer
You are so dear to me

Eekh sheek a sukh liebeh oif dem
veent glykh tzoo deer
I send you a lot of love on the wind, right to you

meet duhnkbehrshuhft glykh tzoo dyn teer
with thankfulness, right to your door.

Dee teer foon dyn hartz
The door of your heart

eekh zeh ohfn oon klohr
I see open and clear

ohngefeelt meet dyn hartzeekeit
filled with your heartfulness.

tahkeh frynd, yohr eebehr yohr
Really friend, year after year,

blyb gebehntcht oon blyb gezoont
stay blessed and stay healthy

meet shmaichlen oif dyneh leepn
with smiles on your lips.

Eekh sheek deer a koosh
meet leebeh oon een fryndshuhft
I send you a kiss
with love and in friendship

myn frynd
my friend,

mineh frynd
my friends,

myneh keendehr, myn fameelieh, myneh ainiklehkh
my children, my family, my grandchildren,

oon ahlleh mentchn een dehr velt!
and all the people in the world.

Meet leebeh, een fryndshuhft, myn frynd, myneh keendehr,
myn fameelieh, myneh ainiklehkh
oon ahlleh mentchn een deur velt! bleibt shehfehdeek
een neshomeh, hartzeek meet
hofenoong!
With love and in friendship, my friend,
my children, my family, my grandchildren,
and all the people in the world.
Stay abundant in soul, heartful with hope.

eech sheek deer a koosh
I send you a kiss.

Namaste, Shalom.

KABBALAH INSIGHTS

The wisdom, and the beauty, and the deep lessons
of Kabbalah are teachings that are referred to as
The Tree of Life.
Ten utterances, it is said in Judaic study,
created the universe.
It is that what God, Adonai, created.

Kehtehr. A divine light of creation
shines in everyone, and on everyone.
Chochmah. Let it shine on wisdom,
experiences in time.
Binah. Then understanding takes it shape
when wisdom and understanding unite
in creating the world. Gentleness arrives.
Chesed. Grace awakens compassion.
Loving kindness. Love, the moral code.
Gevurah. The love that teaches humanity
to not be blinded materially.

When grace, compassion lived unite,
they build another gift indeed.
The mercy that we need, above the
splendour of all consciousness, *Tiferet* exists.
This is the point of your being — knowingness
in the beauty, true beauty of bountiful seeing.

Netzach. Witness our desires expressing feelings here.
Victory aligning them, experiences dear.
Hod. Grandeur, the majesty of thoughts,
God's insight to our vision. Our choosing what serves
best, life, and life's request.
Yesod. The act of power of God's
universal frequencies, a physical, intimate,
spiritual pairing of divine and human worlds,
all sharing. Righteous deeds fulfill the world,
as creators deeds present
opportunities to fill our needs.
Yes, our body and earthly senses,
our planet, the root of the tree.

Malchut, the presence, the lower unites
with the upper, both count.
Original error, cost separation.
We connect, and we repair, and
we ground true awareness.
We are aware of all we can be,
and all we can share
through the Tree of Life
and the Teachings of Kabbalah.

Shalom, my friends.

BEING

Being in our being, we can recognize ourselves
in each other's reflection.
Needing to love unconditionally
and needing to be loved unconditionally.
As beings of brilliance in the phenomenal field
of un-mined greatness, humility,
in the splendour of our world here we are.
Being. This is a gift imbued by energy
Which creates universes, the divine energy
that fashions every aspect of life.

We exist in this miraculous world, together.
We have come into life to develop,
to share new stories and to
honour our ancestors.

Remember to learn from history.
Imagine new vistas out of the innocence,
compassion, intelligence, intuition, flexibility,
joy, beauty, healing, and transformation.
Yes, honouring the past and
looking into each moment
As we move into the future.

This liberation of transforming transcends.
We attend to our own being.
Being in our being and in so doing helping
all other beings.

PROMISE OF THE OCEAN SONG

The ocean song within you,
that fills your every pore.
Just close your ears and listen,
you'll be right there I'm sure.
Find it. Breathe consciously.
Pranayama within you.

For life created ocean and life created you,
so don't forget the motion
there's nothing you can't do
that's meant in life for you.

Rejoice in using knowledge
and feelings to expound
the wealth of life around you.
Let go and you'll have found
silly somethings happening
that might get in the way
of you and your true mission.
Learn and love each day.

By caring deeply for yourself
and all you see and know,
your spirit will embrace you.
Your radiance will glow.

The ocean song within you will grow a rhythm true
And carry you across the waves
Till you come home to you.

EMBODIMENT

Our bodies hold so many feelings,
sometimes we don't know we're concealing.
Experiences, tucked away, and then they rise,
What do you say? What's best to do?
Acknowledge what is going on in you.
Name an emotion, a thought-rising feeling.

And if you do not know, be gentle with yourself.
Find someone you can talk to.
Go for a walk.
Allow yourself to be, embody your healing.

Embodied feelings need to integrate
and sometimes you need
someone else to listen.

Then you'll open insightfully
and see the steps to take rightfully.
Embodied self, make no mistake.
We all have places we could go into our history.
and when there is something that is blocked,
revealing truth, embracing love may truly help
to uncover mystery.

How you show up really counts.
Be loving to yourself.
Embodiment of who you are
requires your embracement of the you
that you let go,
that needs to come back home.
The spirit of your being saying,
"Focus. Do not roam."

Experience is showing you
one of many ways embodied
truth frees you from the haze.
Be free in who you are.
Embodied peace. Embodied joy.
Embodied being.
Shine your star.

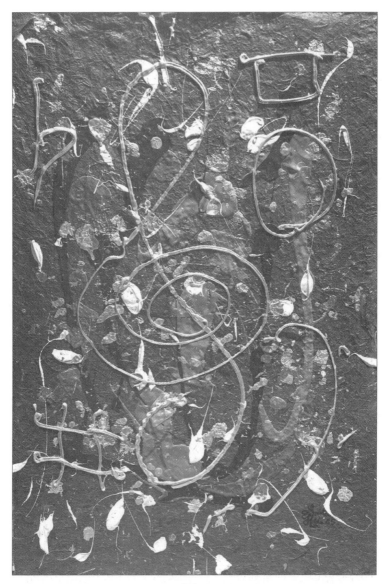

Music

MUSIC

I listen to the music of life.
I hear it in the rests.
In the full circle of life.
In the reminder of that red blood
running through my veins.
The blood within everyone
who is singing a song
of life.

Sunshine sprinkled everywhere
like leaves falling,
leaves growing,
the blue of sky and the waters,
and the gold and silver bounty
of all the elements.

Oh, the music of the mountains and the sea,
and the rivers, the oceans,
and the ever-green of love
in your heart, your body, your mind
and your spirit.

Illumination.
I hear the music
of life.
Listen carefully, joyfully
to the music of life, in each moment.

DEAR SOUL

Our hearts are beating beautifully
because the divine allows.
Brains brighten when spaciousness enters
through stillness, through kindness,
through love, through compassion,
through common sense,
and through creativity.

We become the watcher of
our thoughts and feelings
and as we watch and observe,
we know this to be true—
The Light, the God spark,
the grand nature our spirit
within and around us is felt.
Our soul spirit communicates with us.
We only need to listen.
Our souls are the embodiment
of our Being.

JUST ONCE

Just once you meet someone
and notice something. Just once.
A tilt of chin, a gait, a grin.
A shape of hand, or face.
A shoe, a coat, a posture stance
A generous smile, a pace.

Wide eyes, deep pools of light.
Raven hair, ginger, blond, brown, slender, thick.
How someone moves, the sound of voice.
The way they speak, or make a choice.
Their walking grace, humility.
Their dignity, civility.

A memory forever etched.
Just once you meet
someone
and notice
something.

In your heart, the memory
that makes you smile.

IMAGINATION

Let our imaginations never cease to
create the stories
that imbue our life with meaning.
Creativity and knowing,
shedding as much light as we can
in each moment,
in each magnificent vibrating breath.

Be blessed in this, the knowingness
above, below, within,
reflected in each bless-ed divine soul.
May we all be vessels of purpose and unity
to all that supports a loving, meaningful life.

Let us take flight like a white dove,
blessing our families, our friends, community,
with all we have plenty of.
With this pure light of caring,
here's to our dreams come true
for a loving world, whole
abundant in full view,
where sound values help us live healthfully
adjusting to life and life's throng.

Generation to generation and all our life long.
Li'heetra-ot. Until we meet again.
May our imaginations never cease
to create more love and help bring more peace
to our own lives and all others.
Intelligence alive and well,
we're all sisters and all brothers.
Let our imaginations never cease
to bring out the best in each of us
and into the world.

Shalom. Namaste.

Oh Canada

OH CANADA

Oh Canada, Oh Canada,
hearts of passion rise.
Sunset, morning sunrise, before Canadian eyes
and all who live here.

People who have come to build
a home in this fine land.
A melting of so many hearts
who live to understand.

The Unity. Opportunity. Community.
Oh Canada, Oh Canada,
we stand saluting thee.
Oh Canada, Oh Canada,
a country living free.
Oh Canada, Oh Canada,
a wondrous country too.
May everyone who lives in Canada
bring pride and joy to you, Oh Canada.

Learning from the land we see
the forests and the mountains,
the lakes and streams and rivers.
The ocean and the cities and the towns

Oh Canada, Oh Canada,
forever strong and free.
With love and pure humility
compassion is the key.
Oh Canada.

America

AMERICA

America, America,
the lotus blooms in you.
America, America,
butterfly dreams come true.
America, America
Shakhina,
America,
transforming with whatever is your prayer.

America, America.
Stay strong and blessed and true.
To everyone, America, that lives inside of you.
America, America,
may angels watch and see.
America, America,
your soul, inspired, free.
America, America,
the kundalini flame.
America, America,
meritocracy reclaim.

May every nation live in truth
Of teachings built of love.
America, America, the eagle and the dove.

SACRED SENSUALITY

Sacred sensuality, a reverie of
tenderness, adoration and love
leads to that which serves remembrance
of our bond to life, creating
rituals built out of love.

A bath to fill the senses and relax the body.
A steam or shower, flowing droplets of water.
Life's elixir, relaxing, refreshing,
invigorating the body,
and the mind follows.

Creams, lotions, oils, to gently
massage the body and say,
"I love you," to the gift of the body.
Sacred sensuality, sacred nature.

Sultry summer, inspired spring,
feeling autumn, wondrous winter.
Seasons of our lives in sacred sensuality.
One with the other, and in our solitude.
Sacred sensuality.

TRUE SELF-LOVE

True self love is not selfish.
To care for our whole self,
every part of us is necessary to feel whole.

In nourishing and nurturing our mind
with knowledge,
wisdom,
creativity,
enlightenment,
in honouring our bodies
with
movement,
nourishment,
exercise,
intimacy,
sound and healthful touch,
in honouring our spirits
with nature,
precious
books,
stories and
shared love,
we live the selflessness of love
more ready to share it all in joy and gratitude.

True self-love reminds us of the other
as they are, but a reflection of us,
whole-fully.

LOVE'S FLOW, BODY KNOWS

And body says, live with an illuminated heart
free from jealousy, resentment and anger.
Move into love's flow.

A heart that touches others simply, deeply, is yours.
Cultivate it, feed it with loving warmth,
gentleness in gestures, and expressions.

Allow yourself to fall in love again
with life in action and in silent reverie.
The greater cosmic blessing is operating
all the time, hidden and revealed
to body, mind and spirit.

Give love with ease and sincerity
and watch what happens.
Illuminate yourself and all others
with an awakened body,
an awakened heart of love.

IN BETWEEN THE KISSES

In between the kisses, soft and gentle.
heartfelt, warming.
Our embracing, strong and soulful,
eyes meeting eyes, smiling gracefully
with affection and reflection
in each other's eyes and souls.
Breathing, bountiful and peaceful.
Radiantly, two hearts beating.
Love's assurance, in coherence
in between the kisses, soft and gentle.
Sacred bliss of this being,
in this love, this life, this all.

SENDING LOVE IN BEING

Centred in our being, being with
our body, heart and mind.
Relaxed thoughts, relaxed body,
relaxed heart, relaxed mind.
We can feel, touch, sense, see
and hear the symphony of our being-ness.
Cosmic blessing, lived in peacefulness and love.
We have this love to give, emotionally,
physically, mentally, spiritually.
In sharing love appropriately,
centred in our being, we awaken.
Om, Shalom, Habrakha, the blessing.

The Four Seasons

THE FOUR SEASONS

Spring, Summer, Autumn, Winter.
Each one a world, a gift.
Each one, divine in wonder.
Physical, spiritual, emotional.
The soul of every season,
is deep and filled with joy.
The buds of Spring,
the Summer bounty,
the Autumn glory, colours changing.
Readiness for wondrous Winter.

The beauty of the gem tones of each season,
How they dance, they move, radiating
with life's romance.

Spring's eagerness to
open fresh to the season's will.
And in sweet Summer.
Summer's colours, bright
and full, and sultry sounds.
The splendour of Autumn.
The scents of leaves transforming,
Winds blow,
as various leaves cascade and twirl.
Snowflakes, Winter. Blue skies, sunshine,
pure white blankets everywhere.
The ice, the wind,
then the stillness of a stunning,
sunny Winter day.
Snow melts. Spring again.

EETKHUH METUKAH
WITH YOU SWEETHEART

Eetchuh metukah, uhnee tzreekhah
lalekhet li-okyuhnoos
eetkhuh metukah.
boh-oo naylekh yahd bi-yahd
tuhkluht hayarayuhkh mahlah

With you sweetheart.
I need to go to the ocean with you sweetheart.
Let's walk hand in hand under the full moon.

kisheh-haokyanoos meemlahmahl
alainu bikuhltzuhv shellah

As the ocean murmers to us in her rhythm.

eetkhuh metukah
With you sweetheart

uhnee tzreekhah lalekhet li-okyuhnoos!
I need to go to the ocean
with you sweetheart.
Eetchuh metukah.

THE ARTIST'S OFFERING

Spirit painting, cosmic truth.
Universes all unfolding.
What is it that helps give birth to new ideas
inspirations and creations?

May I write a poem, compose a song,
a melody, a picture to help guide you
to your hidden insight?
Here is private invitation
to the depth and loving joy of you.

With gratitude and latitude
artistically, the writer,
the poet, and the educator.
Heaven-sent you are to me indeed.

I'll paint a picture for you.
A picture of your soul.
The universe supplies the download,
and I am just a servant of the divine
who comes to you in humility and gratitude,
humbled by the enormity of
your wondrous presence.
An artist at heart like you
creating life in each moment.

Childhood innocence that ignites
ego-less states, removes judgment and criticism.

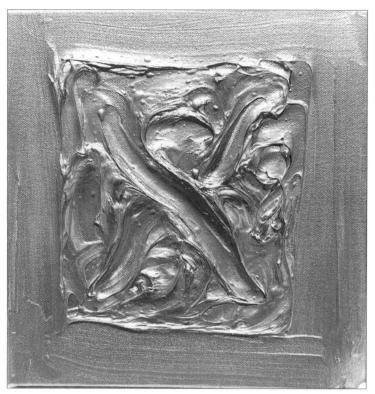

Aleph

ALEPH

The Aleph, the first letter of the Jewish alphabet
brings all worlds together.
The Divine within all.

Aleph is the connector to all the worlds.
The world of possibility, the world of ideas
not yet laid out in a blueprint.
And the world of actual blueprint and design.
And this Earthly world of form.
All four worlds integrated.

All four worlds being lived at once.
Aleph. The heart of it all,
Aleph. The king and queen-liness of
the universe combined as one.
Aleph. Four worlds, like the four seasons
Making up the One.
The Oneness of the Divine
that shines and shines
through space and time
and beyond space and time.
The infinite ... Aleph.

HEALING

Shalom wholeness, peace.
Peace, Love, the Eternal without end.
Ain Sof.
The unspoken name of the divine.
Hashem.
The unspoken name that is felt.
Hashem.
Simkhah! Simkhah. Joy, Joy.
Om Shanti, Om.
Harmony, Peace, Harmony.
Healing. *Marpai.*

CHAKRAS AND SEFIROT

Hindu teachings, energy centres of creation.
Chakras, wheels of energy.
Life force at play.
Each person adjusts theirs
through insight each day.

Sefirot, Kabbalah teachings, energies of creation.
Spheres or vessels of life's attributes
lived every day.
Each person's life story in Sefirot design
to that which are your gifts
and those that are mine.

Together we share in this world
So divine.

These luminous life pathways
clear truth night and day.
These ancient true teachings
give way to love's crown.
For sacred and Godly practical presence
imbues us with learning
and living life's essence.

BEFORE WE SAY GOODBYE

Before we say goodbye, I want you to know
I'm honoured and I'm humbled.

We share this road together,
in spirit, love and being.
Let's stay connected heart to heart
feeling, sensing, seeing one another one day.
And sharing smiles and stories
through laughter, tears, through song and dance,
with walks in forests by a lake,
the ocean, by a mountain,
along a city street or on a country road,
beneath the bodhi tree or in a synagogue,
a temple or a church.

I'll feel a presence, I will know
your voice, a whisper heard.
If I can help beyond a word I've spoken
just let me know

and I will go inside myself

and reach a little further

for what you need in spirit.

DIVINE DOWNLOAD FOR ALL SOULS

From soul spirit to all souls:

"I have loved you long before you came to this Earth,
as you are. You have always been an expression of light,
love, and all possibility to manifest love,
to deepen your connection with your true self,
to witness this within all.
Do not let superficial tendencies erode the true,
beautiful nature of your being.

"Attend to your own birthright of care.
Respect your boundaries and the boundaries of others.
Live freely with compassion,
in health and appreciation,
with creative expression and the genius of you.

"Listen closely to your amazing intuition, igniting your
intelligence, your insight, and your laughter — the
harmony within you. Keep embracing all of you,
all the parts, for you are wholeness, beauty, love,
transformations and stability.

"You are a powerful expression of life and love's
frequencies. Spirit adores you. Spirit loves you.
Dearest one, peace, love, harmony."

Namaste. Shalom.

ACKNOWLEDGEMENTS

I THANK GOD in the synchronicity of life for allowing me to be part of the millions of creative artistic souls who have been given the opportunity to create and share and put into the world their insights through reflective work as I have here. Professionally I want to thank Dr. Lorene Shyba for her guidance and friendship. She is a radiant genius of a woman, wonderful professor, publisher, creator, and so much more. She has provided me with a journey of a new kind of self actualization. Thank you Lorene for opening a door for me to walk through.

Thank you to my sweetheart and life partner Dr. Leonard Smith for providing an environment of unconditional love. Besides encouraging me to keep being who I am, Lenny helped set me on a path that led me to become both a certified international Pranayama yoga teacher and a certified international Chopra Global meditation teacher.

I want to thank Deepak Chopra and the late David Simon, the co-founders of the Chopra Centre, for their lessons as physicians both in Western and Eastern medicine. Knowing you in friendship over the years, sharing in private conversation and exploring depths of consciousness over the years has been highly rewarding.

David Ji, thank you for the learning and growing that you inspired. You were an amazing meditation teacher and business teacher as Dean of Chopra Center University before you embarked on a wonderful program of teachings on your own. Thanks to Dr. Claire Diab who taught yoga at the Center. Thank you for always elevating our awareness as teachers. Thank you to Dr. Sheila Patel, now the medical director of Chopra Global. She and I are colleagues in Primordial Sound Meditation, graduating from the Chopra Center University program together. Thank you to Gabby Forleo for your patience and guidance. To the entire fabulous team that has unfolded and keeps nurturing and supporting teachers globally, thank you.

Thank you to Darlene Quaife, my creative writing teacher at the University of Calgary in the 1980s. Thank you to Sherri-D Wilson, former Calgary poet laureate. I had the joy of performing, introducing many poets and sharing spontaneous creation of poetry for the Spoken Word conferences Sherri-D Wilson has created. Thank you also for supporting this project with your words of inspiration for my work.

Thank you to Dr. Jayashree Bhat and Suresh Bhat for your shared insights to the depth of Vedic teachings and, especially to Jayashree, for your philosophy and the immense beauty of your expert proficiency as a scholar and teacher of East Indian music. Thank you to Eckart Tolle for your inspiration years ago when we would meet in satsang and small gatherings, share ideas about science, healing, spirituality and life in silence and in conversation. Your encouragement then to share my work was inspiring. Thank you to the universe for my serendipitous meeting and individual audience with the Dalai Lama whose hands are as soft as silk and his eyes as penetrating as a laser, holding world knowledge in a case of spirit and being-ness.

As an abstract colourist and cosmic multimedium storyteller painter for decades, I want to thank fellow artists and dear friends Paul Van Ginkel and Kristin Bell for the inspiration and support we share. Paul, I love how we inspire each other as artists and friends and thank you and Kristin for the opportunity to grow and learn in friendship.

Thank you to Shirley MacLaine whose visits and inspiration over a number of years in San Francisco, Vancouver and Calgary were filled with spirit, and influential creativity, artistically and soulfully. Thank you to Michael Flowers who first introduced me to you.

I thank all the students I taught over the years as a teacher in all grades from 1970 into 1996. Thank you to the Akivah Academy and Henry Wisewood High School in Calgary where I presented workshops on personhood and emotional development in adolescence. Thank you to the former I.L. Peretz school in Winnipeg and in Calgary for the opportunity to teach Yiddish, Hebrew, French and English.

Thank you to the gifted pianist Yefim Bronfman, my cousin, who inspires me every time we meet. Thank you to the late Michael Burgess who invited me to be his guest soloist in Winnipeg and Calgary and to be the Santa Baby chanteuse as part of my performance. Thank you to Sister DuPrague my first piano teacher at four years old, in the convent near my house. The sacred experience of hearing the gentle whispers of the nuns away from the piano room was mystical too.

Thank you to Kathleen Van Mourik and Charles Foreman for co-creating Mountain View Festival of Song and Chamber Music and inviting me to be your guest artist for two concerts. Kathleen, you prepared with me and accompanied me so beautifully in your brilliance. The program was a tribute to liberation in Holland, and the Second World War. Thank you for asking me to do a complete program of Yiddish, Hebrew, and English.

Thank you to Jewish Family Services where I have been called upon for over four decades to give concerts for seniors at seniors residences.

Thank you to Cantor Alex Stein for allowing me to sing the beautiful prayer for peace in Israel on several occasions, at Beth Tzedec. Thank you to Rabbi Leibl Wolf, whose classes and personal inspiration have continued to imbue me in Kabbalah wealth and Torah teachings from a deeply Orthodox perspective. Thank you to Rabbi Matusof, Rabbi Groner, their families, and all their wonderful Torah classes. You teach what I grew up with at home. Thank you to the late Rabbi Shachter, Rabbi Jordon Goldson, Rabbi Mark Glickman, Rabbi Ofseyer, Rabbi Shechter of blessed memory, Rabbi Weitzman, Rabbi Corber, and Rabbi Alan Green. You continue to inspire me with what you teach me. Thank you also to Father Dubois and your amazing work.

Thank you to my amazing parents Rachel and Mendel Szternfeld. My conversations and unconditional support continues to sustain me while you are physically gone. Thank you to my precious daughters Penny and Mandy who light my life beyond words, together with my grandsons Caleb and Zane. I love you all so much. To all my cousins near and far, thank you, and a special thank you to my Auntie Barbara. My cousins in Winnipeg, Sharon, Elliott, Yonah, and Libby were and are like siblings to me. Last but not least, thank you to my sister Debbie and her beautiful family and to Lenny's brother Stan and his family. All the people I have mentioned and more are what inspire me to stay tethered to the sacredness of relationship, writings, poetry and the fuel that fills my desire to share love and its blessings as a teacher and ambassador of wellbeing through my work for those I can be of service to in this world.

Thank you to all not mentioned. You live in my heart. You know who you are.

Shalom and *Namaste* to your health and wellbeing.

Hilda Chasia Smith

CHASIA

Hilda Chasia Szternfeld Smith was born in Winnipeg, Manitoba, Canada to survivors of the Holocaust. Her middle name Chasia was given in remembrance of her aunt Chasia Goszer who died in the Holocaust. Hilda Chasia was a self-realized child; filled with wonder and curiosity, which led her to express a true love of the arts, music and education. She has taught Hebrew, Yiddish, French, and English languages, charm school, music, art, meditation and yoga. She holds degrees from The University of Calgary, The University of Manitoba, Chopra Center University, California, and Pranayama Centers International, founded by Swami Vignanananda. She was part of the Women's Writing Project at the University of Calgary and has contributed to the Literary International Reading Association (LIRA) writings on Poetry in the Classroom. Her poetry has been published in the *Winnipeg Jewish Post* and the *Calgary Jewish Star* and her paintings have been represented by galleries in Calgary, Alberta and Winnipeg, Manitoba.

DURVILE &
UpRoute Books

Other Books in the Every River Literary Series

Series Editor: Lorene Shyba

A Wake in the Undertow: Rumble House Poems
Rich Theroux & Jessica Szabo

_____

Living in the Tall Grass: Poems of Reconciliation
Chief R. Stacey Laforme

_____

Vistas of the West: Poems and Visuals of Nature
Foreword: Doris Daley
Editors/Curators:
Lawrence Kapustka, Susan Kristoferson, Lorene Shyba

_____

Umbilicus: Poetry and Visuals of the Sensuous
Carrie Schiffler & Johanna Stickland

_____